Unweaving the Web of Trauma

Copyright © 2023

All rights reserved. No part of this publication may be reproduced, distributed, or transmitted in any form or by any means, including photocopying, recording, or other electronic or mechanical methods, without the prior written permission of the publisher, except in the case of brief quotations embodied in critical reviews and certain other noncommercial uses permitted by copyright law.

Book Design by HMDpublishing

2023 book cover artwork designed by Yamuna Savini

A guided tour through my personal life events.

Unweaving the web of trauma through consciously locating the headquarters of where my patterns and behaviors stem from. Learning to transmute what doesn't bring me joy and what wasn't mine to keep in the first place. Through this deep self dissection, I have given myself permission to heal and forgive myself and others. This daily practice assists me in reframing how I communicate to the universe and what I create through this conscious communication.

We are worthy of freedom, peace and harmony, but it is our conscious responsibility to attain this level of awareness.

Contents

Consciously creating our reality 1

Acknowledgement 2

"Whoop her ass." 4

"My creation elixir was radiating through my body." 15

"Can I borrow a chess piece?" 22

"We don't want to die; we want versions of ourselves that no longer serve us to die." 30

"You confronted your attacker." 41

"Everyone who chooses to have kids is selfish." 48

"I almost died from an oven exploding in my face." 56

"My best friend doesn't shake—she twitches." 62

"What we give energetically is energetically given back to us." 70

"We are the universe." 76

Consciously creating our reality

We are the creators of our reality, and by adding more tools to our toolbox, we can begin living our highest timeline.

The gift of creation is a conscious choice rooted in daily conscious practices.

Consciously choosing to embody love and be void of judgment or projection when interacting with any other being is our foundation for truth and light.

Nobody hurts us; nothing we experience is the fault of another. We are the creators, and what challenges we designed in our soul contract are divine. We designed every detail of our human experience—no mistakes, no accidents: all pure intention. We are souls having a human experience here to grow and learn how to embody the love frequency to the fullest. No matter how hard it seems, we designed it this way because we are strong and our courageous souls are here for a mission.

Acknowledgement

I am writing this book for me, for my children and the children that follow.

I'm writing this book for every courageous soul who is choosing the path of enlightenment, the path of evolving ourselves from the generational learned behaviors of guardians who weren't strong enough to face these truths before us. Guardians who were not provided a safe environment to grow into their most authentic self.

My truths in this offering stem from drastically evolving my belief systems, in myself, in this world and in who we are in this human game.

I began writing this book at 8 weeks pregnant with my first child. While I am in deep self reflection of who I am and how I reached this timeline. I am feeling every emotion and learning this new version of myself. I am cocooning in my home as I unlock these new realizations of what it is to evolve from maiden to mother.

I am writing this book as a reminder of how far I've come without forgetting what molded me and who alongside myself I am healing in my bloodline.

What we heal in ourselves we heal in others.

What we do to improve ourselves isn't for us; it's for the children. For the children who will enter this plane of existence with a mission to change the world. Not only our birth children but every child whose soul chooses to come Earthside. What legacy we create for ourselves will be the information that inspires them to create their own legacy.

To every person I mention in this offering, you are a major character in my human experience. You did exactly as I needed you to do for me to become the woman I am today. For me to evolve my consciousness and expand my awareness of what powers I hold. Thank you for your contribution to my journey. I love you and I forgive you for what you did while you were in your own human experience as I also forgive myself.

"Whoop her ass."

The majority of a human's personality is created through learned behavior. What energy we embody and exude as a parent or guardian is the behavior our children will reflect until they have acquired enough life experience to reframe their behaviors which would require them to do their own shadow work which in most cases involves them doing the healing that the guardians weren't strong enough to face. Does this sound familiar? Does this feel like a generational circumstance you recognized in your guardians? Let me share my personal awareness of this situation.

I was raised by Angie, a suffering, aggressive, addicted woman who was raised by Rita, a suffering, aggressive alcoholic woman. Angie made it very clear that if her four daughters were alive and she was mostly present in our reality, then her children were living a better life than she did. This truth she held would convince her that she was a better mother than hers based on her "better behavior".

Angie did, in fact, live a horribly sad and troubling childhood that makes mine look rather mild, but comparing trauma leads nowhere and doesn't make one experience "easier" than another when it comes to how we as humans each store trauma in our cell memory and the influence trauma has on our life choices.

Rita chose drinking which led to her successful suicide at age 65. Angie didn't want to be like her mother, so she chose meth and chooses it to this day at her age, which is damn near 65.

I didn't want to be like my mother so I chose cocaine, Adderall, promiscuity and alcohol. Unlike Rita and Angie, though, I consciously chose to clear out my shadow and call my learned behaviors to light to feel them and heal them. I continue to choose this daily; it is a daily choice to face ourselves and our generational darkness to keep those ancestral voices heard but without giving them power to influence how we operate in our daily lives.

This is just one awareness, and it comes with many segways to a multitude of other behaviors. This is what I call my headquarters of my lower vibrational patterns, stemming from this one generational behavior. There are many more with more and also less power that have the potential to influence my daily patterns and choices, which is why I consciously practice self love and self acceptance daily.

Every new sunrise I check myself before I could wreck myself. I practice energetic hygiene every second and call my darkness to light before it consumes me and drops my energy down where I would be sitting in my own pile of shit. We are no good to ourselves and others if we drop down into our lower vibrational patterns. We must call them up to light and manage them through a higher vibrational lens. Dropping into the low vibe would look like becoming a victim to our thoughts instead of neutrally observing them: asking ourselves, "Thought, why are you here? What darkness is asking to be seen or heard?" This practice can keep us operating in a high vibration where managing such questions is way easier than if we are sitting in them, feeling sorry for ourselves.

A common new age claim labeled "disassociating" is what I hear people say when they are processing their truths. I would like to add that I don't agree with this word or its energy. The truth is you are processing your shit and you don't have energy to give external situations your attention. This is valid! This is healing! This is a beautiful awareness that when communicated to your surroundings: "I am processing some information; please have grace for me while I am with myself" is an amazing way to uphold your energetic hygiene.

Energetic hygiene also looks like checking yourself before you enter into a public space or gather with others. A low frequency choice would be to sit with others and drop your low vibe energy into their fields in hopes that they will become your source of happiness or "fix" you. This is poor energetic hygiene, this is energy siphoning and you should check yourself before making this your go-to pattern.

Also learning how to spot this behavior in others is an expanded awareness. Bringing the choice to light in a neutral way is also a beautiful awareness. "I acknowledge that you are processing something and I am here for you but please don't dump your energy on me, just ask for my guidance, and if I have the capacity I am happy to be of service to you."

Due to my courageous decision to call the learned generational behavior of addiction to light, I am consciously preparing my child's world to be trauma free from this darkness of addiction.

My conscious choice creates a ripple effect that reaches every family member, especially my sister's children, who are also faced with the possibility of this generational behavior pattern. My sisters and I carry this energy from both sides of our guardians. It is a huge responsibility to consciously choose health and peace over all forms of addiction, to be of service for the generations that follow.

Behaviors can be as big as addiction or as small as frustration. Something I also experienced in child-hood. I learned to be pissed off when something didn't work. I learned that if someone took too long with a food order, then we should bitch about it. That if a car got in front of us, we should cuss and yell and honk because we are entitled to be in a rage energy.

I was verbally commanded to "whoop her ass" if anyone at school messed with me, and I did this regularly. Angie would tell us girls, "If you come home and you've gotten your ass whooped, then you'll be getting another ass whoopin' when you get home."

This truth I believed firmly, so I followed directions. I also witnessed Angie "whoop the ass" of a mother from the opposing team during one of my soccer games when I was at an impressionable age of 8. This woman was verbally abusing my best friend on my team with hateful words about her weight, telling her to "get off the field and go eat a hamburger." It was vile and, well, little did she know my mother grew up on the east side and had a nut button that was always on the edge of popping. There I was, dribbling down the field when I heard shouting and turned to find said woman getting her face smashed in by Angie.

I cried a lot. I was scared of how I would be punished by my coach or how the soccer league would treat me. I was mortified because my best friend from school was also there for this one freaking game and her family were hardcore Christians, an incredibly soft and naive family, and we had to face her family after this game.

Our relationship declined greatly after this experience and for good reason; I believe they knew that Angie wasn't the world's greatest mother since she would leave me at their house for days without so much as a phone call to check on me. Regardless, my friendship was damaged from this incident.

I was innocent and enjoyed peace until at age 12 when I would begin viewing the world through a darker lens.

Angie often choked us girls, slapped us, threw us into walls. We sisters abused each other as well. This aggression was a very normal part of our life until age 30—I hit my last human, I fought my last fight and I projected my last bit of rage onto another human, and that human was Angie.

This was the last and final moment I accepted myself as an aggressive woman. Every bit of pain, suffering, fear and anger I had had since childhood was released that day onto the woman who inflicted the most pain onto me. I choked her, I threw her against a wall and I hit her just as she did me. When I was finished I looked at her and asked, "How does it feel? This is exactly what we received our whole life. You will never hurt me again."

I walked away feeling nothing. I walked away, and from that day until now and for always, I finalized my contract with my female portal. I forgive her and I forgive myself. I have immense gratitude for her because she did exactly what she needed to do in her human experience for me to learn from and grow from. She sacrificed herself this lifetime in so many low vibrational ways so I could become the woman I am today. So I could clear these generational traumas and create a new bloodline void of addiction, void of aggression and void of shame, guilt and anger.

This action of me returning the behavior did not serve my conscious expansion, but the ramifications of me choosing to match her energy that day was a huge catalyst for me choosing this depth of healing. There are no mistakes in life. From that action, I decided I would prioritize my peace, which meant removing contact with Angie. I decided I would stop fighting others and start loving myself enough to embody calm and peace. I decided I would heal the gaping wounds that were memories replaying like a tape, influencing my actions, influencing my patterns. Influencing my relationships.

I consciously chose to clean out my dark closet that hoarded my anger towards her abuse. I decided to view her as a broken child, never being heard or cared for with proper love and nurturing. I made the conscious choice to forgive her, consciously knowing that she is a projection of her sad, suffering inner child who did to me what was done to her.

This experience I share can be considered rather extreme. Not all learned behaviors come with such force. Some of our learned behaviors can be perceived as smaller and more innocent, like taking something from another that is theirs without them knowing. Maybe your mom had sticky fingers when you went to Grandma's house and you learned that if it's family it's not actually stealing.

But all things done behind the back of another are in darkness. If you can't share it aloud out of shame or guilt or knowing you'll get in trouble, then it is shadow energy.

Or maybe your dad would call in to his boss and say he was sick but then go play golf. This is shadow energy; this is what guilty parties call "little white lies". These accumulate and take up space in our closet. These little bits of darkness compound, creating overpowering little devils that sit on a shoulder telling you to take your dad's wallet, steal your grandma's pain pills, bully kids at school.

Little white lies are not little at all. They are pieces to the puzzle that when placed together tightly with others can create explosions of guilt and shame, which are super low vibrations keeping your spirit in a low frequency, magnetizing to you many more low vibrational carrots just dangling in front of you. In this energy at this vibration, you are creating a storm of like-minded peers. Our vibration creates our company. We are who we hang out with.

To teach one thing and do the opposite is also living in darkness. If you say "stealing isn't kind" but lie to the drive-through lady about your order to get a free taco, then you're in darkness. If you tell your kids "no junk food in our house", but you are grabbing the chips when the kids are sleeping, that is living in darkness. Yes, even if they don't know about it, you are harboring a shadow energy. If we feel shame and guilt about saying it aloud to anyone and everyone than that is living in darkness.

Our shadow houses our lower vibrational choices. This is an energy that is very loud and heavily armed. When it comes to darkness, there is no big or small, and all of it holds power over us; if we are choosing the conscious path of enlightenment, we must operate fully in the light. To be fully enlightened, we must be fully of the light.

When we reach an age or enter into experiencing life where we are operating from our own consciousness, being responsible for our own choices which create our own patterns, then it becomes our responsibility to start cleaning up the energetic shit we inherited from our guardians. It's our responsibility to clean out the closet and decide what is trash and how to dispose of it properly to prevent it from being recycled. We don't get to straddle the fence and keep some behaviors out of our ego who claims them as "personality." We have to fully surrender to the conscious choices of preparing the path for trauma-free, karma-free children. "Its not our fault that we are fucked up, but it is our fault if we stay fucked up." A quote from the book You Are a Badass.

One of our most powerful human superpowers is the ability to create another human life, to be the portal through which another chosen soul gets to enter the human game. The preparation for such an event begins when we become conscious of our own choices. The moment we start living our truths and unplug from the mental enslavement of the 3D world and rewire our beliefs to our unity consciousness truths, we will begin paving a path for the generations who follow us.

No matter what age we are or where we are in our human experience, we can start our conscious creation to become a divine, sovereign portal. If we are not creating a timeline where we create a human, we are still responsible for creating a reality where the children are free to think and be whomever they wish to be. Just one of us, choosing sovereignty and choosing to manage our trauma and be clear that our Karma is raising the collective vibration for the generations that follow.

A conscious guardian then has the grace and compassion to encourage their child to begin being incredibly mindful of their actions towards others and how karma is created. A conscious guardian living in the light would encourage their child to accept their energetic contribution in every situation they experience. These conscious guardians would have embodied truth and light in all ways so the child can grow in a safe environment to be themselves authentically and unapologetically.

This is an ideal scenario for how we prepare for the generations that follow us. You are most likely the one who is on the path to creating these types of humans and this style of environment, and for that I honor you. It is never too late to become a conscious guardian. It's never too late to reframe our leadership choices or reframe our personal behaviors. It is always a great time to evolve our beliefs to evolve how we show up in the world every new sunrise. We are aunts, uncles, sisters and brothers, neighbors and friends of children; our contribution to the children in our lives is just as important as if we had birthed them ourselves. Conscious leadership starts with conscious humans taking conscious responsibility for their choices, thus creating conscious little humans who grow to be powerful, loving conscious pioneers in the New Earth energy.

"My creation elixir was radiating through my body."

Consciously creating with our sexual nectar is a highly powerful practice and greatly underrated. The human vessel is perfectly designed with everything we need to step into our role as creator and begin playing the human game like a boss. First we gotta clean up the damage we have done to our energetic body. Clean up the residue of the energies lingering in our divine energetic field.

What I am sharing here is lost knowledge; this information has been diluted through decades of grooming humans to sexualize quite literally everything in the 3D world.

To choose conscious creation requires cleansing of sexual energy from all lovers, all sexualizing of others, ourselves and also inanimate objects.

Purifying our sexual energy to reclaim our creation power, to harmonize our creator abilities. This purification process requires each portal, male and female, to temporarily discontinue sexual actions, to discontinue sexual pleasures and be fully entranced with themselves in absorbing the creation elixir that we hold most commonly in our root energy pillar. In the 3D world, we are programmed to freely give away our creation elixir. This can be through porn, casual sex, hooking up, dating apps, masturbation to others, sex work, erotic flirtation, teasing, etc.

If you are dating yourself while holding the vibration of creating family and evolving into parenthood as a timeline you wish to align to, please be mindful to stay present and only concern yourself with your practice. Meaning do not invest your energy into worrying about if anyone else as your potential partners are out there also purifying themselves.

We tend to get fixated on a personal practice and drop into fear that through our evolution, we will not have many options to align with others. The fear frequency is not a frequency we want to hang out in. We cannot create from this consciousness level. Trust the divine magnetization of the universal law of attracting what we are and stay focused within, not without.

You can be creating this timeline through your personal purification and fully trust that your divine partner is also doing the same to prepare for this grand creation process as well. If you are not envisioning a timeline with children, you will still very much benefit from this purification process. You are expressing to the universe that you are serious about partnership and serious about loving yourself to not expect anyone else to do this for you.

If you are already in your relationship, this is a powerful and beautiful practice to share in together. You can introduce celibacy to your meditation and mindfulness with the intention of reclaiming power from anyone or anything you've given your sexual energy to, i.e. porn, previous lovers, celebrities, sexualizing other humans, masturbating to another human, sexual trauma, sexual guilt or shame. All and more of these can be cleansed and cleared through refraining from sex for any amount of time while you both work separately and together to heal your trauma around sex and clean the residue of previous lovers.

It is best to begin this practice without attaching a linear time frame to it. We cannot do multidimensional work while cleaning and clearing energy and attach the 3D construct of time to it. We must surrender to the process and remain present to have grace and compassion for ourselves during this healing process.

The external world is riddled with the sexualizing of literally everything—foods, clothing, any advertisement that is in some way "selling sex"—because the human programming is groomed to respond to sex. When we awaken to our conscious responsibility, we typically find ourselves recognizing shame and guilt around our flippant sexual offerings to anyone who caressed our need for attention when we weren't giving it to ourselves.

We can reclaim this power and cleanse our creation elixir, No amount of lower expression is too much; no amount of shameful events or patterns are too much for this process. We must embody grace for our old identity and the choices we made while we were unconscious of our actions. We can rebirth every aspect of ourselves through self love.

When I began purifying my sexual energy, I wasn't fixated on purification as my outcome. I was simply choosing to be more loving to my body, mind and spirit. I was loving deeply on myself, and this purification came naturally during meditation.

First, I consciously chose to absorb any sexual energy I was externalizing. I recognized how I was flirting with others to fulfill some need of external validation, but I had no intention of acting on this. I just wanted attention, which told me I was pushing out a thirsty vibe which activated feelings of shame and embarrassment.

These are common energies that will surface. We must not attach to these energies, these feelings. It will not serve our ascension to sit in that lower vibrational energy; simply choose to feel it and let it go, reminding ourselves we are not those choices we made while we were hurt and suffering. We are not those patterns we created while in pain and feeling unworthy of pure love and affection. Acknowledge the feelings and choose forgiveness so we can continue our ascension path.

During this time of loving on myself and processing my old sexual patterns, I decided I no longer wanted to pleasure myself with a toy or my hands. I wanted to feel the arousal and gather it and absorb it up my spine out of my root area. I naturally knew I was holding sexual energy only in my root, and the best way I knew of was to "release" it through masturbation, but that now felt wasteful to me.

This is when I began absorbing my sexual energy, breathing it in deeply, raising the energy from my lower energy pillars into my higher chakras. In place of releasing my creation elixir, I was utilizing this energy. I was keeping my powerful juices in me and not throwing them out like dirty bath water.

This changed the game for how I interacted with others. This action of feeling the arousal and working with it was filling me with strength. To reframe intense programming of self pleasure or seeking external pleasure was empowering.

I felt like I was disrupting the 3D program and breaking through an energetic cord that had been passed through my family and all of society. The images of being forced to experience sexual acts around family members that left me feeling unsafe as a child were beginning to fade.

I was absolutely reclaiming my power back from the lower dimensional sexual agenda. I was breaking the energetic chains. I was freeing myself from this trauma and in turn freeing the generations that follow me. When I interacted in the world, I was lighter and more open to communication. I was without the walls I had built to protect me from unwanted attention. I was free from the thirst of seeking external attention from men and women.

I was simply existing in purity and harmony. I recognized myself in the mirror but with much more grace for myself. I started looking at myself through the lens of self love and self acceptance. I accepted the lines that I was previously hiding through botox. I replaced judgment of my body for love and admiration for my evolved womanly curves. I began seeing past the physical vessel of others and looking into their souls. I recognized how others were seeing me as a soul and not my physical form. I was creating deeper connections with friends that I once analyzed for their "partner abilities." I was finally free of lifetimes of sexualization and generations of sexual learned behaviors. I felt exponentially lighter.

With this reclaimed power I began working together with my creation elixir and creating my highest timeline. The 10 year visions I had of living on a farm on the top of a mountain in the jungle started to materialize. My creation elixir was radiating through my vessel, supporting my grandest dreams and working with me to align me to my highest timeline.

I felt purer; I felt reborn and whole. I felt safer to receive and share love, I felt safer to call in my partner. Through my purification, I felt I had healed generations of sexually abused ancestors. I felt them honoring me for this work, and I was proud to be of service in this way. I knew this work I was doing was freeing my children from this karma.

I continued my purification process for about a year and half, and it was exhilarating. I had amazing energy, and my favorite part was how pure my encounters were with the opposite sex. I felt proud of myself and honored to be exuding this purity. I felt the weight of all of my sexual partners or situations dissolve. I transmuted shame and guilt of myself for allowing people to have access to my creation elixir.

My relationship with myself flourished, and to this day I proudly hold the energy of self acceptance. When judgmental thoughts enter, I acknowledge them and gently transmute them with words of love ("I am perfect as I am, I love this version of me"), acknowledging the voice of my ego but reassuring her that we are safe in our skin, we are safe to love ourself as we are and we do not need to change anything ("I am healthy and happy, I love how I care deeply for my body and soul"). I look in the mirror and feel proud of my experienced shape. I feel proud of my body's ability to be active while I walk the acres of land we have, I feel proud and confident that I am a 40-year-young woman who is carrying a healthy baby and living a healthy lifestyle free of addiction, free of lower vibrational patterns and matrix medicine and matrix food. I accept myself and forgive myself for the choices I made when I was suffering, when I was hurting and therefore I hurt others and myself.

"CAN I BORROW A CHESS PIECE?"

Through this process of purification my cell memory unlocked many memories of events that altered my self love and encouraged the lower vibrational patterns of having an open door policy to my sexual energy. One of the most interesting memories was of when I became a woman and how traumatizing it was for me. I had never examined this moment but as I healed my womb and my sexual energy pillar I saw deeper into this and how it is a commonly traumatizing experience for young girls and how it shapes our view of ourselves, our body and our worth.

I was in 8th grade just months into starting a new school, and I was frozen in a bathroom stall looking down at a pool of blood in my pants. I was perched on a toilet in a crowded bathroom full of "popular girls". I was like a helpless child completely unaware of how to manage this situation. I finally found the courage to use my voice and ask for help. I saw an arm reach under my stall and hand me a tampon saying, "If you ever need one, just ask to borrow a chess piece."

The girls laughed and I sat wondering, "Are they fucking with me?" I soon realized this was the underground name for a tampon and it was created so the girls could speak openly in an inconspicuous way to discuss our natural female production. This secret name was obviously designed out of shame so we wouldn't have to endure the disgust that would spew from the mouths of the boys when one of us were required to borrow a tampon from another girl who was in the "period club".

Once my chemically bleached cloth stopper was inserted and my jeans were cleaned up to the best of my ability, I rushed to the office phone to call Angie for support, to share this news with her and ask for more materials to perform my tasks in the track meet that was rapidly approaching. Angie couldn't be bothered to come to school to bring me products; she wasn't a bit concerned with my emotions, and I was reminded how this was a conversation we had never had. I recognized that this conversation was the first one of its kind. I was reminded of the times I witnessed her inserting a tampon but never hearing words of wisdom coming from her mouth. I was sad, discouraged and empty. Even at 13, after the endless disappointments in her ability to mother, I was still hurt by her actions.

This life changing moment came with absolutely zero preparation. I was blindsided, I was embarrassed, I was scared. To add fuel to the fire, it was my first track meet at my new school, and I ran hurdles. Hurdles, y'all. I was so completely uneducated on how these feminine products worked, I was crippled with fear that my tampon would fall out while I was running.

I was convinced there would be a bloody trail following me around the track like I had been mauled by a pack of wild hyenas.

I outsourced my fear and asked a friend to monitor my leaps and strides; I suppose her responsibility would have been to clean up behind me. Honestly, I don't know what I expected of her, but she came through like a champ for me. She ran the whole track next to me, supporting my race to womanhood.

This same friend's dad drove me home after the meet and when I exited the car I had left a red stain on his car seat. I was mortified. He was kind and patient with me. I don't remember this friend's name, but I remember this day and these feelings like it was yesterday. This is the power of trauma. It leaves a lingering residue replaying in our patterns and influencing our self love and self acceptance until we feel it to heal it.

Even after that day Angie still never discussed periods or feminine product knowledge with me. She didn't acknowledge the significance of this huge moment in my human experience. Surely, she treated this situation as her mother treated her—if her mother was even around for this event in her life. Rita came and left often, leaving her children to fight for food and to dig in dumpsters in an attempt to relieve their hunger.

The traumatizing menstruation experience is a common theme for many women. This is such an easy fix that we must be responsible for. Even if you are a single father, please have this discussion with your daughter. She may be embarrassed at the time but when the moment presents itself, she will be so grateful you recognized her. Even if you direct her on who to call or what to do, any communication is better than her being blindsided by a pool of blood in her pants. You can be her hero in this situation just by expressing you are aware of this beautiful moment when a young girl becomes a young woman.

We must reframe this experience; we must clear the karma around menstruation and remove the low vibrational stigma that the peers of these young women are programmed with. If you are a parent of boys, share this beautiful moment with them. Tell them to support their friends or girlfriends, teaching them how to honor this magical expression of womanhood. Through this portal of womanhood is how their children will be born, how your grandchildren will enter Earthside. This is a legitimate trauma that many women carry with them until they do a form of cleansing or clearing of that deep sadness and trauma from this day. I believe how we respond to our menstruation based on learned behavior is how we cherish and honor our womb and our evolution into becoming powerful, confident women. I also believe it's how we accept treatment from the male company in our lives.

Do we accept their immature disgust and embody shame for our natural bodily functions or do we stand confident in our womanhood and verbally command respect?

For me, I accepted the disgusted energy that was projected towards me because I had immense shame around this natural function of being a female. The shame was implanted the day I started my menstruation and wasn't healed until I was 37 years young and sat in ceremony to cleanse this traumatizing experience and rebirth a new energy that radiated gratitude, love and respect for my female functions, for the power of being a woman and I forgave every man or boy and Angie for the shame I accepted as truth that was projected from their unconscious mind.

As I write this and connect the shame from menstruation to the purification process, I see now why that trauma was unlocked during the healing of my sexual energy. I recognize the relationship between sexual trauma and womanly trauma. Our sexual trauma will always show itself in our womb, and from the young age of 13 at the time of becoming a woman, I also received intense cramps and very painful periods to the point of being bedridden and unable to attend school. I was also sexually molested as a young child and experienced traumatizing sexual exchanges from many family members in my younger years.

I believe now that I harbored fear of becoming a woman and who might be attracted to me because of this new maturing phase in my life. I was afraid of attention to my body, which was very developed. The only way I could combat this fear was to submit to it. This involved me growing more into flirtation and giving and getting attention from boys and befriending the more "exotic" girls and evolving from naive child to brave and bold bitch. It was my coping skill to ensure I would be in control of who touched me and when and how. If I engaged in the attention, then I could control it, so my ego told herself.

These remembrances are when I started developing my desire for rebelling, for getting into trouble and projecting an energy that says "don't fuck with me". This energy definitely protected me in some regard, but simultaneously, it magnetized to me the "bad boys" and the bad choices which lead to the low vibrational patterns I adapted into my lifestyle until becoming consciously responsible for managing these patterns and reframing them.

This conscious responsibility didn't develop until my late 30s, which meant I had a lot of shit to unpack and forgive myself for. I was now responsible for managing the vague memories of being molested at age 2 by Angie's meth dealer to the vague memories of having drunken sex with what's his name from a dating app. I was reminded by my sister of our childhood molestation, and it activated my cell memory, which began releasing other events my ego had hidden from my memory as a way to protect me from those emotions during intense traumatizing events.

Essentially, I had blacked out a huge chunk of my childhood as self perseverance to get me through life. So when this molestation occurring at age 2 was activated, my cell memory unleashed many more stored events, creating a tornado of unmanaged emotions. This is how the trauma healing cookie crumbles, like a busted pipe spewing out emotions that were lodged deep in our cell memory. Clogging up our energetic field and preventing us from embodying peace. Once we start folding back the layers, the truths start unraveling.

Luckily, we meet this level of deep healing and evolution when we are safe to begin this process. When we are awakened to our abilities to be of service to ourselves and when we awaken to this, we will do just about anything to heal. For me, I started my plant medicine journey and utilized any tools from the plant world to expand my awareness and build my relationship with myself. I did this all alone and it was intense. This healing process is what empowered me to be a guide for others who are also on the path of enlightenment, on the path of self discovery and evolving our souls.

My tool box is full of beautiful awarenesses that I implement into my personal self love practices and how I share my truths with others. Choosing the soul evolution path is intense and requires immense courage and motivation to be the very best version of ourselves no matter what we uncover about our human experience. What we heal in ourselves, we heal in our bloodline. When we choose to acknowledge our contribution to every situation, we will recognize the root and begin to master our healing journey.

When we begin self mastery we align to "creator", when we embody the higher dimensional truth that we create every single detail of our human experience, we can then begin shifting timelines. Yes, even my molestation at age 2, I created for myself to experience in this lifetime. I created every single detail of my life that created trauma for me to manage so I could become the woman I am today. So I could evolve my soul in this Earth university we choose to enter into to remember lower vibrational emotions.

We are here for exactly this. I chose all of this so I could sit with anyone needing support and be available to connect with them. My mission is to heal myself first and take these tools to assist others in their journey. I am grateful for my experiences so I can be of service to everyone.

"We don't want to die; we want versions of ourselves that no longer serve us to die."

The filtering out process of which patterns stay and which need to be reframed requires us to dissect this current timeline and, if possible, our parallel timelines as well. Our parallel timelines are created through the choices we make in our current reality and are operating simultaneously to this one, influencing our choices and our reality. These parallel timelines can be dissected through remembering our dreams. When we are making the bold choice to begin this healing process, we are also claiming that how we are living and functioning is not acceptable for our highest timeline.

This evolutionary process is a path that leads to a temporary state of solitude. We begin shedding versions of ourselves that no longer serve this new frequency, we shed patterns that are tasteless to us, we shed people who operate at a lower frequency, we shed aspects of ourselves that do not match the timeline we are envisioning for ourselves. This shedding creates a death energy, and the majority of us will enter into our "dark night of the soul".

This is a place of deep self reflection where every painful feeling of self doubt rises for us to feel it and heal it. In the DNOTS, we often have suicidal thoughts because we are so depleted by the lower vibrational energy we are purging that we want to end it. What I have learned from my personal experience is that we don't actually want to die; we want the pieces of ourselves that are no longer serving us to die. We are grieving our old identity and going through the greatest death process to be reborn into our next best self.

This process is heavy through one lens and fucking gorgeous through another. I entered my DNOTS in late 2018 after a major car accident that left me without a home, a vehicle and without a strong body to work on my hair clients, and obviously, I was left with immense trauma. I was driving my truck and pulling my 1969 Airstream trailer down a crowded two lane highway when the world's tiniest car entered my lane, driving head on towards me. I was able to slow down a bit before turning the wheel to the right, entering the shoulder while he did the same because that was the only place either of us could go. We collided with his front right side hitting my front right side, sending his car spinning out of control and breaking into tiny pieces while I came to a stop just inches before a cattle fence.

To my surprise, I was upright and my dogs were completely fine. Immediately, I began panicking at the horror that whoever was in that car was dead. I was driving a Ford F-250 pulling a 31-foot travel trailer—essentially, I was a semi—and this tiny car hit me going at least 80 mph while I was able to slow to about 50mph. Unable to move from pain, I yelled to the witness who was standing at my window "check on the people in the other car; I think they're dead."

It was all happening so fast, and the world was spinning around me, I couldn't get grounded. The man returned with a young 21-year-old-guy who was entirely too calm and unconcerned about this situation and was also the driver of the world's tiniest car that had just hit me. I became furious, which snapped me into reality. My body was shaking and yelling for me to sit, but I was in shock; how was this guy and his buddy unharmed, so much so that they were laughing and kicking around the dismembered bumper. I felt like I was imploding. The 911 operator encouraged me to sit down and remain calm.

I was 2.5 hours from my hometown, but they wanted to take me to a hospital 2 hours the other direction. I declined and took the only other option, which was pack my 2 dogs and myself into the tow truck and ride the painful bumpy trip to the wrecker just minutes from my sister's house where I would be staying.

This wreck left me with 5 bulging discs in my lower back and a horribly bruised ego. I lost my identity; I was the badass who could travel the country alone towing her airstream while operating a very successful hair business. I was the badass who could tow her 31-foot trailer anywhere and set it up all by herself. I was all of these facades because the truth was, that lifestyle was tearing me apart. I was angry at having to do everything alone, I was pissed off at men because nobody would help me without me asking for it, I was so fucking tired of being so strong all the damn time. I created this event. I was drowning in sadness and wishing someone would save me, but instead, I ended up saving myself. I didn't know it at the time, but I absolutely saved myself that day.

From this accident I was left homeless due to my airstream being my home and lived in a hotel for a month before a dear friend's mom allowed me to stay in her house while she was away 90% of the month. I was dropping further down to rock bottom, waking up in my best friend's high school bedroom. Losing 70% of my clientele because my body hurt too bad to work. Drinking more alcohol because it was all I could do to get through the day.

I was turning the dark corner and thinking a lot about suicide. It was a constant thought about how everything I was feeling and the trauma that was surfacing from this event was too much for me to handle. The only logical choice was to end it, but I had tried that before, and that attempt replayed over and over. Seeing my sister so sad and recalling how much pain she felt. I couldn't do that to her or my nieces and nephews. I couldn't bitch out like that and selfishly end my life because I didn't have the tools to manage my trauma, manage my emotions.

I shared this dark thought with a close friend which brought my darkness to light; I was acknowledging this as a true energy which allowed me to dissect it. It allowed me to own this thought and begin reframing it. Just me sharing the thought of suicide awakened my ability to begin managing this lower vibration thought pattern. I began an internal mission to bring awareness to suicide and wanted to offer the world an evolved view of why people make this choice. This mission was my therapy, and even though it dissolved when my low vibrational attachment to ending my life dissolved, it was still a beautiful form of therapy to evolve me through that place. During this DNOTS is when I was presented with the idea of moving to Costa Rica. I didn't think; I just said, "I'm going," and this became my fuel for peace. This was my goal and exactly what I needed to reset my life. Where I once viewed my life as "everything was taken from me" I reframed to "everything is available to me". This frequency is higher than the other, so I began shifting my energy and shifting my emotions to begin creating a more beautiful reality.

I began working energetically to heal my body, and I found relief. I created a couple of side gigs to make money for the move, like opening an online vintage clothing shop, which was so fun for me, and I did well. "My clients left me" was reframed to "I have more energy and space to do other things I love". I was still drinking, popping Adderall and smoking cigarettes, but I knew those were patterns I would face eventually; I was highly aware they were not serving me.

Life events create parallel timelines through attaching emotion to energy. We can have thoughts and allow them to pass, but when we attach emotion to them, we create our reality. Thoughts are energy; everything is energy, and how we respond to life and what vibration or emotion we have attached to it will absolutely create our reality and parallel realities.

This is also how Karma is created, which I believe we get to manage in our dreamstate. What Karma we create in this waking reality creates parallel realities where a version of ourselves is living out that karma. When we rest this vessel, our consciousness works on the other realities to manage those timelines.

It's like when we have huge fears around, let's say, getting attacked walking to your car in a dark parking lot, this thought attached with emotion creates a parallel timeline where this can occur. When you go into a dream state, you will live out these fears in ways similar but also matching that frequency.

The best way to create our reality is to be highly mindful of our thought patterns and reframe them immediately. When this fear enters your thought pattern, breathe and reframe it by saying, "I am divinely protected." The more we say it, the more we believe it. This frequency is higher than the frequency of fear, so we can begin dissolving the fear timelines. This is how we start shifting our timelines.

During my processing of the car accident, I was not as consciously aware as I am today of how I was managing this traumatic event of the car accident. I was accepting that my body required rest, and the reduction in my clientele was a gift for me. A gift offering space to care for myself and feel everything that surfaced from this event.

I went through anger towards this kid that I continuously reframed from "this dumb ass kid was in a hurry and did this to me" to "an inexperienced driver made a poor choice and luckily I was attentive, which saved our lives." This reframing freed my body from holding onto that low vibration of hate and anger which was keeping my back in pain. This reframing allowed me to see how this event was a situation I created because I was so miserable going down a road of self destruction.

This awareness and forgiveness for him paved the way for me to forgive myself for the thoughts of wanting to kill myself. For the first time in my life I was allowing myself to feel the current emotions which was allowing me to process the event without storing the trauma inside my energetic body or physical body. In the linear time of about six months, I had processed the event and also managed the emotions of the event.

This realization after the fact is crazy amazing. For the first time in my life I sat with the pain, anger, fear, sadness etc. and processed it. I managed the emotions which eliminated the trauma from storing itself in my body. I am aware that how I was able and willing to manage this event prepared me to begin managing any events that would occur from here on out.

The car event unlocked a new level for me which gave me power to start healing all of my trauma. I had shifted my fear of facing my shadow energy to motivation to clear out all of the debris. I was ready to reclaim my power and face the new world I was creating. I stopped making choices out of fear of feeling trapped emotions and started making choices that made me uncomfortable about the possibilities of the outcome. I stopped protecting myself from feeling and I started empowering myself through healing.

This cycle of "protecting" ourselves from feeling our stored emotions will create a barrier preventing us from deeply dissecting our contracted events. The best way to begin this dissecting process is to begin with the most recent patterns that we recognize are not serving us. Once we can accept our lower vibrational choices and make the bold choice to face them, to heal them, we can make higher frequency choices to evolve out of them.

When we dissolve one pattern—let's use excessive drinking as one—we are freeing up energy for us to cleanse our energetic field of this low vibration, simultaneously raising our vibration and allowing us to see more clearly how this pattern had many low vibrational choices stemming from it.

This alone may be someone's headquarters, but we do not as kids decide drinking a bottle of vodka is what brings us joy. This definitely may be a learned behavior from guardians or society, but it is not the root; it is an outcome of a root, it is the low vibrational solution for the symptoms of trauma. There are probably multiple headquarters that require deep dissecting leading to the drinking, but it is still recommend that you dissect what patterns stem from this low vibe choice.

A good way to envision this practice is the writing web we used in grade school English when learning to write stories.

When we decide at some point in our life to drink bottles of vodka or endless shots of tequila, we commonly do so to numb ourselves from the trauma we have yet to manage, typically due to not having a safe environment to deeply feel this level of darkness.

For me, I drank to escape the pressure I had placed on myself to perform in my leadership position of owning a hair salon. I drank because it paired perfectly with Adderall, and I drank because my ego told me I deserve it when completing a "busy day at work". I then drank during work because I was so worn out from life that I really didn't care and with enough Adderall in my system, I was never getting drunk; I was staying in a perfectly numbed state while mixing the Addy with the booze.

This cocktail was my fuel for managing life when I wasn't managing my emotions or the heavy load of trauma I had stored in my vessel over the 37 years of being Earthside. Drinking wasn't the headquarters of anything for me because stopping drinking came very easily when I entered into a safe environment. Choosing to drink excessively wasn't the root; drinking was the "fix" to the root. The headquarters was my obsession with proving I am not who my parents are. My obsession to perform and be seen by the world. I would beg to say my Adderall consumption was more of a root problem than my drinking; the more I popped Addy the more I drank. The more I wanted to prove my abilities to the world, the more Addy I popped. The more Addy I popped, the more I created extra projects for myself to complete for external validation. It's a spiral of unhealthy low vibrational patterns.

This is a form of dissecting, tracing the root and analyzing how we gave our power away to it. Once we target the root, we can dissolve the energy around it by reclaiming our power and ceasing the siphoning of our energy from said root.

Who we allow access to our energy and who we allow to take up space in our reality is also a root concern, it is also a pattern. Trace each relationship, platonic or romantic, and you'll find a common theme amongst them all. Some are designed by our choices and some are designed by our soul contract and our female and male portals. Regardless of their origin, we are responsible for managing every place and person we have relationships with.

"You Confronted Your Attacker."

Making the courageous decision to heal from trauma is our greatest testament to consciously accepting the role of leader. Consciously facing all of our darkness, not only for ourselves but with the mindfulness of preparing a karma-free timeline for the generations that follow us. The less shit these generations have to manage, the more they can focus on their mission, the more they can embody love energy to offer their superpowers to the world. If we are working to align to the timeline of birthing children or being a guardian, then we must be consciously responsible for ourselves even when children of our own are just a thought in a timeline we envision. What we heal in ourselves, we heal energetically through our bloodline.

When I was a young girl, I was very vibrant and unique, I carried a playful energy that made every- one laugh. I also carried a highly mature "old soul" energy that often had adults questioning their existence and tilting their heads in skepticism trying to "understand" me. I was often creating skits or playing in the dirt digging for worms. My stepdad and Angie moved us through at least 25 houses until I was 17 years young, when I left home for good, standing firm in forbidding either of them from controlling me into moving back home when they decided to put on their parental hats.

I first moved out when I was 14 and lived a happier life with my aunt and uncle until the age of 16 when, as a punishment for my public display of singing Baby Got Back to my sister at her wedding and "being an embarrassment" to my stepdad's family, he pulled me out of work and out of my aunt's house forcing me back into their meth lab of a home to "teach me how to be a respectable child".

This was short-lived due to their increasing meth addiction and the exploding garage that moonlit as a meth lab. I resentfully retreated to my older sister's house, where I would live until escaping my hometown two weeks after high school graduation to travel the US, following around jam bands while heavily experimenting with psychedelics.

Through my childhood years, I experienced an unstable family dysfunction of super highs and super lows. A higher time like when my parents were holding down jobs and making good money, which coincided with me getting diagnosed with a tumor in my right fibula.

Now, I see how having a tumor does not compute as a "high", but having the stability of money was something so unique that it did at that time relieve me of some stress to know if I needed something they could afford it. They weren't able to sympathize with me or physically care for me, but to compensate for their emotional neglect, they performed tasks like taking me on shopping sprees. At this time in my life, I was easily manipulated by this money because it was something rare for us. I was in so much pain and so scared of this emergency surgery and how it would affect my love for soccer that I accepted any form of bribery and distraction.

While I was in this vulnerable state, I do believe I thought the shopping and outings were an acceptable display of love and affection. It was the best they knew how to do; an unconscious mind cannot display levels of affection required to calm a suffering child during such a traumatic life- changing event.

The tumor was removed and found to be benign, but the recovery was 9 months, and that was a brutal 9 months for me and my mental state. The last month of my recovery, I was invited to join my best friend and her family to Disney Land, where I would get to enjoy myself walking without crutches and living life for the first time in 9 months. I was so excited to treat this as a celebration of healing, but the truth is, I was angry and depressed with how destroyed my leg was and how weak I was.

We had a joyful time and when we returned I kept the celebration alive, while my best friend and I went to a college party with her uncle, who was 27 at the time. I remember what I was wearing: a button-up white shirt tied over my belly and my other friend's pair of Abercrombie jeans. I remember we took shots as soon as we arrived, and after that, the night went dark.

The next memory I have is riding in my friend's car, passed out and waking up to her taking me home to my sister's house. The next morning I awoke to my alarm, which was set to prepare for the weekend trip I was taking with another friend while she went to singing competitions. As I wiped from my morning pee, I saw a long pubic hair on the toilet paper. I didn't have pubic hair; I shaved completely. Immediately, I received flashbacks of the night before of me hanging my head in the toilet and my friend's uncle coming to check on me, moving my limp body from the bathroom to his bed and then a memory of our bodies on top of each other.

Fear and panic started arising, but I shook it off so I could get ready for my trip. I was in a state of disbelief. I know I only had one shot, so how did I get so drunk? I didn't feel hungover, so what the hell was going on?

After the first night of being away, I decided I had to tell the friend I was with what happened. She encouraged me to tell my sister and get a rape test when we got back. By the time we returned, it had been over 72 hours, so there wasn't enough evidence in the rape test to make a strong case against him. I was so angry with myself that I didn't keep the pubic hair.

I told my other friend whose uncle it was and she wouldn't, or couldn't, believe me. I went to a detective, and when this went public, I had many other women contact my sister to share their story of how he had also drugged and raped them, but none of them would testify against him in court.

This was how my 9 month recovery ended and this is also how I entered one of the darkest times of my life. I didn't leave my house for months; I couldn't even walk outside because my anxiety was so bad. I was coloring and drawing like a child, doing the best I could to live each day. I was having panic attacks daily or multiple times a day. I cycled through therapists and received the typical western medical system fix of matrix medicine that I refused to take but would be the full prescription I would consume the morning I attempted suicide.

My rapist, let's call him Hunter, received what I call a ghetto form of punishment from my sister's very aggressive guy friends, who were like big brothers to me. They found him and hurt him every chance they got, but no amount of pain inflicted on him relieved the pain I was feeling.

Eventually, not too long after his string of attacks, he moved out of town. My greatest defender met him in a crowded bar many years later, and Hunter begged for his life to not receive another beating. He begged, "Please, man, I have a family, I have kids." My defender replied, "Do you have a little girl?" Hunter answered him with a terrifying "yes" and the last words he heard were, "I hope you never have to experience your daughter feeling the pain you have caused so many young women."

These words must have reached into his soul and penetrated some depth of regret, but his lessons from this event are not my responsibility.

I have forgiven Hunter, not because he deserves it, but because I deserve it. I am grateful for that event and the dark emotions that surfaced that required me to heal and grow from it. I am grateful because now I get to be of service to anyone who has also experienced this abuse. As a baby of age two, I was molested and as a 17-year-young woman, I was raped. As a 20-year-young woman, I escaped another attacker and again while I was on the beach in my said paradise, I escaped two attackers.

The last time I was sexually abused was the day I was walking with my dog Zuna one early morning on the beach and this guy was sitting on the sand. I passed him and turned around to see what he was doing to find him standing upright with his penis in his hand masturbating. He then proceeded to follow me down the beach until I yelled out for help. He rushed back to his rental house, and I raced off the beach to my house.

I knew he was a tourist because just the day before at sunset, I had crossed paths with his family and exchanged hellos. I was furious at this little punk, Fuck you for doing this at me. Fuck you for selfishly projecting your filthy sexual energy into my peaceful morning. Fuck you for coming onto my beach, my happy place, and showing me your nasty dick.

I was fed up with these encounters, so I gathered myself and I drove directly over to the house where he and his family were staying, interrupting his mother's morning by sharing the whole story in detail about her son's public display of masturbation and how there were two little girls playing in the sea just 50 feet from his selfish act. I expressed how selfish it was for him and how this act would probably not be his last if he didn't feel some form of punishment or, at best, embarrassment from it. He stood in a room upstairs above his mother and me while I expressed myself in detail, remaining hidden in that room, listening and denying the whole scenario.

His mother didn't seem shocked enough for me to believe this was the first time they were presented with something like this. I walked away with my head high and my shoulders back.

When I turned the corner out of the property, I heard a strong voice within me say, "You confronted your attacker." I immediately began to cry. I didn't confront just this one guy, but by my action to confront this kid, I confronted every lower vibrational energy inside of me that held onto any of my sexual abuse experiences. I took action to release this sexual trauma from cycling through my existence, and I transmuted it with my choice to confront it, which shifted any energy influencing this timeline or any parallel to this one.

"Everyone who chooses to have kids is selfish."

In the 3D frequency, there's an energetic equilibrium that is essentially a law that tips the scale and needs to balance out our highs with lows. This is the 3D world that our human self chose to enter so we could have these challenges to grow from and learn from. This is also more of our childhood truth because we are essentially under the karmic spells of our guardians. How they are living their lives is influencing our personal experiences. When we reach conscious expansion and become responsible for our actions, we can then choose to live only in highs, aka ascension. What we are projecting is what we are receiving.

Now, let me get really clear on how I am categorizing everything I just shared in the previous chapter as a "high". This determination is coming from my younger, more naive mind of living a life where I wasn't sure when I would see my parents for days or if my older sister and I would be caring for our sisters and how long we would be without our guardians or if they were even alive.

I was familiar with us relocating houses every other month. So when they were present because they were sober and were making a solid income, yes, this felt like a high.

Angie was present with me almost everyday while I was waiting for my surgery. I was living with my aunt and uncle, but Angie was there to take me out of school when I was on medical leave and needed to be homeschooled. She was with me every time I remember hitting the ground and being paralyzed in pain from the tumor shooting up my leg and into my back. For this traumatic life event, Angie was actually there and as a "poor kid", her having money to feed me and take me shopping was a super high.

One of my lowest moments that presented itself was when I was 13 and escaped my house through a bedroom window to flee the scene of my step dad carrying a giant butcher knife through the house. I suppose he was awaiting the arrival of my meth-induced mother, who had been MIA for days. While my stepdad was making his rounds through the house, I quietly jumped out of my first story window to safety from the terrifying situation.

This was a somber self rescue mission because I had chosen to save myself while my two younger sisters were still in the house with him. I was certain he wouldn't harm them because they were his blood children and he loved them very much. He and I struggled terribly to live in peace; since day one, I had such hate for him. I wanted my dad, and nobody else could compare, even though my dad was also quite elusive during my childhood and the majority of my adult life.

Once I was out of my yard and safely in my aunt's get-away vehicle, I raced to the house of my mother's friend in search of Angie. Here I found her, only to learn she was there but didn't want to see me. Turns out this friend was also their drug dealer and the family I would babysit for while I was 13 years young, and on multiple occasions, the two kids and I would be left alone for 24-48 hours with only a handful of money and commanded to order pizza any time we were hungry. Neither set of parents would check on us; they would just return once they were done partying.

These moments and the residue from them shaped my perspective of life. These experiences along with my organic knowing that the 3D world we lived in was suspiciously corrupt. Starting at a young age and until a few years ago when I awoke to the truths of the human game, "Fuck the system" was a common phrase spewing from my mouth hole. These life experiences that molded my lens of life also supported my strong conviction to never ever want to have children. Another common phrase was, "I would never bring a child into this dark hell of a world. Everyone who chooses to have kids is selfish."

Obviously, I was viewing the world through the lens of a victim and as a child of such challenging experiences, it was valid. It is valid until we consciously awaken to our responsibilities of being our own healer and reclaiming our power back from anyone and everyone who contributed to dismantling our innocence.

It was at age 37 when I met a partner—let's call him Neal. He poetically recited all of the things to stroke my spiritual ego. He serenaded me with a highly conscious vocabulary, and we engaged in deep cosmic conversations. It was while we were karmically entangled (aka in a partnership) that I opened myself up to the idea of becoming a mother. I don't recall really ever thinking he would be the perfect partner or a perfect father figure, but I'm grateful his presence rubbed my maternal instinct and I began adjusting my lens of motherhood.

Neal's role in my life was beautiful and guided me into healing many timelines of hatred towards myself and the world. His presence guided me to opening my heart to motherhood and choosing to dissolve old beliefs of living in a dark world. My perspective now of this human experience, this Earth university, is that it is beyond beautiful, it's our responsibility to come to this conclusion. We are here in this human game to evolve our belief systems—this is how consciousness expands. It's entirely more alarming to stay fixated in one truth for eternity when we are playing a game that we are solely in charge of. We are the main characters in our own simulation so lets start leading like it.

I recognize how divine my soul contract is and how Angie is the perfect example of how I don't want to mother. She lived in constant fear and self- hatred while also being a full blown narcissist. She loved her four daughters when it was good for her personal show. She showed up to my MVP traveling soccer games because I was the star, but when it was a simple high school soccer game and I wasn't the star, she couldn't be bothered. As I grow more conscious and view everything through the lens of acceptance and truth that we are all here controlling our own simulation, I have zero low vibe energy towards her or my life experiences with her as my guardian.

Having Angie as a reference to mothering, I am highly inspired to be the best mom ever. At one point I was so invested in motherhood I was completely accepting of doing it solo;, needing nothing but a suitable sperm donor. This was a timeline I would have accepted as "enough", but the timeline I was truly envisioning and working to align with was a beautiful family with a very supportive papa—the ultimate opposite of what my inner child experienced; this would be the medicine that would fully heal my bloodline from these generational learned behaviors.

Neal and I finalized our contract after only 3 months of him moving to Costa Rica with me and 6 months of us being an unhealthy karmic couple. It ended in aggression from him, projecting his anger onto me because he was so incredibly miserable being out of his comfort zone, which was our hometown and his immediate family. Is he to blame? Absolutely not! When he yelled at me, I yelled back for a while.

After sitting with Mama Aya and burying my old identity, I no longer matched his energy of rage. This rage energy would be his demise in my new reality. Me not matching his energy increased his rage, and I became fearful of what he might do to me or my dogs. I was so peaceful after my Ayahuasca ceremonies that I had no more anger. I had no more hate that could fuel such rage. I am very aware of my contribution to aligning with this man. I once had immense anger and rage and could yell back or fight with him.

In the beginning, I sought out security in him; after all, we met as I was coming out of my dark night of the soul. I pulled out my amazing artistic skills and painted a fictional picture of how perfect we were together, damn well knowing his relationship with his mother would not jive with our new Pura Vida lifestyle. They Facetimed multiple times a day, and he had a standard to live up to that they assigned for him. I appreciate and honor family, but this was an obvious unhealthy attachment. They knew one version of him, and I knew another. They knew who he pretended to be to keep them happy, and I knew the version of him that he displayed in an attempt to keep me happy.

So many characteristics of him and our relationship were eerily similar to my first marriage. Super conservative Christian parents with a son who envied me for my authenticity, all the while him playing a character for both sides until he popped.

See, I had this pattern where I would magnetize "Mamas boys" to me—it was infuriating until, of course, I accepted the truth: these men were perfectly playing their role for me to learn my lessons, another truth being that we attract what we are or what we need to recognize within ourselves.

I was vibrating to the unhealed wound of the absence of a mother's love and the dark perspective of choosing to disown her. He was vibrating to the smothering of a mother's love and people-pleasing his family and others. Do you see the equal vibration there and how what I was feeling would attract this behavior?

This attraction was shining the light on my unforgiveness for the inability of Angie meeting my standard of what the label I define "mother" to be. The "mother" label is simply that—just a 3D label given to our female portals. A label that causes immense grief for both the portal and the child when either of them don't perform to the standard of what the other's definition is of this label.

Angie's definition of "mother" is drastically different from mine. Her daughters are alive and living good lives, so in Angie's mind, she fulfilled her mission. When we can view our female portals as humans and not create ownership of them meeting our or societal standards of their given label, then we can finally enter into forgiveness.

One of Neal's roles in my human experience was to reflect to me the areas in which I was failing to accept my contribution to what was preventing me from evolving. We were a couple when I exited my DNOTS, and we were a couple when I entered my next highest timeline of living in Costa Rica. He played his role perfectly for me to awaken to my lower vibrational patterns and the many parallel timelines I was creating with these characters that would continually influence my current reality if I didn't make drastic changes in how I lived my life. Drastic changes in how I managed my stored trauma. His presence was a pivotal moment in me shifting timelines from angry maiden to softened, compassionate mother.

Neal would not be the last one I magnetized to me. Oh, no, there were a few others after him that were very short-lived. The universe, aka ourselves, always repeats patterns to be super duper sure we have learned from the experience. These men were huge messengers telling me to go deeper into my healing of the mother wound and deeper into softening. I continued to work on myself, and I continued to evolve my personal standards and my standards for whom I allow access to my energy. Most importantly, I moved deeper into self love. Yay for growth!

"I ALMOST DIED FROM AN OVEN EXPLODING IN MY FACE."

We have choices in life, many choices, but we also have egos. They are strong and they love comfort; comfort is safety for them. Safety is what we trained our ego to control for us. The ego steps in the first moment we feel emotions that alarm our nervous system, that set our emotions on high. The ego begins being constructed and perfected through each moment where our environment feels unsafe and our human emotions get turned way up. The ego is our bodyguard, and we are who we are and where we are in life because of our ego. I am so grateful for my ego; because of her, I am alive today. Because of her, at age 17, I yelled for help after downing a whole bottle of antidepressants in hopes of ending my suffering.

My ego presented a strength and determination to the external world which allowed me to own a successful salon while also internally drowning of sadness, grief, resentment, anger, guilt and shame. My ego and my heavy prescription of

Adderall are how I kept myself functioning. The other option was to manage my trauma, and that assignment was entirely too grand for me while also caring for a team of other people and being fully engaged with my clients and their personal life. These excuses kept me safe, and my ego liked that. Unsafe would have been to feel all of the stored emotions I chose to hide deep in my body in place of feeling them from every single traumatic event I experienced.

The idea of quitting my daily routine of drinking bottles of wine and dirty vodka martinis to numb myself, smoking ½ a pack American Spirits and popping 90-100 milligrams of Adderall was just too much to even consider while I was still living in the 3D world.

Every morning my alarm went off, I swallowed the Adderall placed strategically next to my bed. I return to rest until the next alarm which was strategically timed for when the Addy would kick in. I rose and started my day with a glass of champagne or wine. I filled up my Yeti cup with wine and walked out the door to work where there was always more wine in the fridge for when my Yeti ran dry.

I was operating in the world while consuming all of this, so therefore, I was fine. This routine enhanced the closer I got to leaving my dusty old Texas town and moving to the Caribbean. It was like "going out with a bang".

My ego also empowered me to take the biggest chance of my life: leaving my comfort zone with a pretty mild savings account and the courage to create a life that would set my soul on fire. I was moving to another country, and my ego was absolutely not going to accept defeat of this challenge.

I entered Costa Rica, the happiest country in the world, on September 11th 2019.

It sure as shit felt like an emergency. I was doing serious damage to my body, mind and spirit. I still wasn't completely convinced that I had a problem that needed fixed, though, until September 22nd 2019, only 11 days after arriving in Paradise. I was in my typical work mode of "get shit done" while working on the property I shared with my business partner, her boyfriend and Neal. We had an Airbnb that Neal and I were responsible for redesigning for our guests who would surely be flocking in to stay with us. I was energetically invested and monetarily invested; so much so that I skipped the beach and got straight to work. After all, that is what the Adderall told me to do; I couldn't dare waste the Addy energy. So while I was high on Addy and floating through the garden, I was reheating food in our gas oven. I ran to check on it, hoping it wasn't burnt only to find it was cold and the oven wasn't lit. I grabbed a lighter, knelt down on the floor, facing the oven to light it, and BAM! the 30 minutes of running gas exploded in my face, throwing me 6 feet across the room.

As you can imagine, I was shook. I screamed the most horrific scream. I was quickly greeted by Neal, who was confused as to why I was freaking out. I was confused as to why he wasn't freaking out.

Commanding a mirror to inspect the damage I, quickly realized my face wasn't melted off, which revived my ability to take action in healing myself.

I healed myself for 7 short yet grueling days of energetic surgery, meditation and cycling through a combination of intuitive medicine concoctions. The seventh night, I celebrated my strength and healing abilities by throwing my 90-day prescription of Adderall into the fire and never thought again about that disgusting drug. This drug was the cause of this terrifying event, but still I felt such gratitude for the situation. I felt deep emotional gratitude for this moment where I chose to blend my low vibe choices into my new high vibe environment which led to the death of a seven-year addiction. In this case, some would typically say, "The universe was looking out for you," but I know that I am the universe; we are the universe expressing ourselves in human form.

We as the universe create scenarios that revolve around our belief systems and reflect our inner truths. My belief when moving to Costa Rica was that I was going to heal myself; I was moving here to kill the versions of me that no longer served my highest timeline. I moved here to become a version of myself that loved herself and loved her life. This Adderall addiction did not support that timeline, so it had to go.

I as the universe created a drastic scenario that would rock me to my core. A scenario that would scare the shit out of me so badly that the action alone would rewire my neural pathways. This moment was exactly what I needed to enter into the next best version of myself. This event also disrupted the stories I was telling myself of why I should stay in my unhealthy karmic relationship with Neal.

When we choose to recognize life events as beautiful creations for our growth instead of shit that happens to us, then we can evolve and learn. We must be responsible for shifting our mindset from victim to victor. "I healed myself in 7 days from second degree burns" vibrates much higher than "I almost died from an oven exploding in my face". No I didn't — I survived something that woke my ass up from the dark shadows where I had been hiding.

Shifting our mindset is how we shift timelines; it's how we expand into higher consciousness. Shifting our perspective of our personal life events relieves us of the stories we create of the suffering we are experiencing from life events. If it isn't happening in the now, then it is a story. So we must be responsible for rewriting these stories. My old Adderall story was "I'm so busy; if I don't have it, then I can't complete my tasks." The true story was "I am jacked up on synthetic meth and I'm creating projects to absorb this crackhead energy".

I forgive myself for choosing Adderall and damaging my perfect human vessel with this poison. I forgive myself for influencing my sister to participate in the meth mind. I forgive myself for creating many other low vibrational patterns stemming from the Adderall headquarters.

These seven days of healing unlocked for me the remembrance of my powers, who I am as a natural healer. This event activated my motivation to not just get my body healthier, but my energetic body, my mind and my spirit. I took drastic action to improve my life after this event. This event dissolved many timelines created by the Adderall headquarters. This event shifted me into a much higher timeline where I was reconnected with my abilities to see into other dimensions, to reach into information that would assist myself and others in their human journey. What we heal in this current self we heal in other timelines.

"My best friend doesn't shake—she twitches."

Age 17 was a doozy for me; I created some incredible challenges for myself in that year. I grew a tumor, I discontinued my passion for soccer, I experienced rape. I also lost my virginity that year, and it was far from beautiful.

One of the hardest moments though was when the year was coming to an end, I buried my best friend, my uncle Harvey, the uncle I lived with when I left my parents house at age 14. He was the only father figure I had, and we were so close. I was the last person he saw before his transcendence.

This experience would drastically change my view of myself and my view of life. After learning of his transcendence, I locked myself in my bedroom and mourned for days. I didn't know how I would go on without him. He was the only one who was consistent for me. He did what he said, and he always made sure I was taken care of even if we had to hide our relationship from my aunt, Angie's sister, who was jealous of our bond. He wasn't even my blood relative—he never married my aunt— and yet he showed me more attention and love than any other parental figure in my life. We made it an every other day event to go out together for lunch or dinner, and when I needed school supplies or new soccer shoes, he was always the one coming through for me. The days after his transcendence, I would have a lot of contact with him. The days, weeks, months and years after his transcendence, we would still communicate. He was my protector on both sides, and this was the beginning of my communication with the other side.

I had, since a young child, witnessed supernatural occurrences that never scared me. I was told by Rita that I shared her psychic gifts, and she and I were oddly close; even when everyone misunderstood her, we were weird together.

Age 17 would change my trajectory for who I was becoming in this magical Human University. Unbeknownst to me, this cycle would come back around every 5 linear years and would present life-changing moments for me to learn from and grow from.

Age 12 was a year that disrupted my innocence and reframed my hope to hopelessness, and the little bit of joy I was holding was rewired to resentment. I shifted from 6th grade student council president to a dark shadow; every glimmer of childlike wonder I had was erased through the events that would occur in my 12th year. As I said before, I was a daddy's girl, but he was hardly available for me. I would learn at age 30 it was due to Angie's aggressive behavior and confrontational personality that kept him away. She was so difficult that his submissive energy was too damaged to fight with her anymore, so he gave up.

As a 12-year-old girl, all I knew was that he didn't want to see me. One night he had promised to pick me up and let me stay with him at my grandma's house. I watched out of our living room window for hours, awaiting his arrival. When it was around 9pm, I was completely discouraged but holding some hope when my stepdad entered the room and said, "Your dad's a piece of shit; he's not coming to get you."

This shot pains into my heart, and on this night, I entered a new realm of existence. On this night, something inside of me died. I would never be the same, and my entire human vessel began malfunctioning because of it.

First it was my stomach. I would scream in pain and unable to eat anything or properly use the bathroom. Angie took me to doctors, and I was diagnosed with my first bleeding ulcer. I was put on a strict diet and prescribed matrix medicine.

At age 14, I would be diagnosed with a second bleeding ulcer. This stomach problem wouldn't be solved until age 28 with a completely different diagnosis.

A couple months after the ulcer diagnosis, I developed a twitch that started with excessively blinking my eyes and within weeks terrorized my whole body. I had just started my 7th grade year in junior high, and practically immediately, I was unable to perform school tasks. I was twitching so badly, my school teachers were concerned and were exempting me from writing, reading aloud and typing class. I was too weak to participate in athletics. I was badly bullied for this but with so many close friends near me, they were so concerned that they protected me. They stood up for me.

I recall perfectly in typing class while I was sitting aside, not able to participate and receiving hurtful words from the class, my best friend stood up and yelled, "My best friend doesn't shake—she twitches!"

This was a funny moment and I remember having grace for myself. I was a confident young girl, so I don't recall really becoming too invested in the bullying. My home life was shit, so I had bigger things to concern myself with.

I eventually reached a place where walking wasn't possible. I was hospitalized and monitored 24/7, unable to leave my bed, peeing in a bed pan and being cared for as a toddler. I was being fed, clothed and bathed by someone else. Angie was there; she was with me for the majority of my hospital stay.

Who never showed up, not once, was my dad. Again I would learn at age 30 that he would not not show up, even though he was the only person I was asking for.

Angie, as narcissists do, controlled the whole scene. She was loving the attention she was getting from the concern of the doctors. Narcissists operate like this; they thrive when they can be energetically filled up through any form of attention. I believe she knew that having him there would help me and soothe me, but that wouldn't benefit her.

After 2 weeks of around the clock monitoring, I was released without a diagnosis. I was sent away to live with Angie and my stepdad in this condition. This twitching would stay with me until about age 37, and even now I have moments where I twitch in certain ways which are commonly related to my breath.

I didn't receive a matrix diagnosis because the western medical system isn't programmed to identify and manage energetic ailments. I now know, through deep self reflection and meditation that what I created was an energetic malfunction from the trauma I endured as a child and the absence of my father was the straw that broke the camel's back. I manifested this physical twitch in my energetic body, and it lingered until I healed myself of the trauma that had compounded relentlessly in my life.

I am aware now and hold immense gratitude for these life events, even though my inner child was horribly discouraged and required intense repairs. Through the healing of my trauma, I also sat inside myself and listened to the voice of my inner child. In every memory that would occur during meditation, I became the guardian, the safe space, and soothed that little girl in those moments. Through this practice, I would dissolve and clear timelines that were influencing my actions and patterns in my now reality.

I was grateful to befriend my father at age 30 and create a safe space for him to share vulnerably with my sister and me about the truths of his absence. We were able to share with him how these moments altered our human path, and we were all able to grow a bit closer that day.

I love my dad and believe he has one of the purest hearts I know. I believe he harbors deep pain, sadness and suffering for the unmanaged trauma he also endured, but he never created a safe space to process these traumas. I see him for the loving young man who also had a very challenging childhood and is crippled by unmanaged emotions. He became a father at age 17 and was energetically corded to an aggressive narcissistic woman. I forgive him for submitting instead of fighting for us. I forgive him because he did and is doing the best he can with the level of self love and level of consciousness he has.

We don't talk much or really at all. He lives a somber life in a state of victimhood with his wife, who also has a meth addiction. I can't be certain that she is living in this addiction currently, but something tells me they are trauma bonding and sharing in their low vibrational patterns together like they have historically. My dad was never a big drug addict—he loves his weed, and he once loved drinking beer, but last I heard he discontinued that due to multiple DUIs and probation.

I created my female and male portals to be heavily armed with addiction and unhealed trauma. My soul entered through their portals, knowing and accepting our combined contracted mission for me to be the one who clears the karma, manages the trauma and breaks the generational behaviors. For this to be successful I needed them to be as low vibrational as possible.

My conscious expansion is reliant on how much I learn through this lifetime in this current vessel. I believe I am a much more evolved soul, which is why I took the responsibility of enduring their karmic patterns in childhood and in my experienced years, learning from them who I am not. It is quite rare to have more than one highly conscious soul in the immediate family or even the bloodline who is currently participating in the human game.

I believe this is evolving through the great awakening, which is cycling us through our higher dimensional evolution. What we heal in ourselves we heal in our bloodline. The life I am creating, free of low vibe karmic patterns, free of low vibe generational behaviors and free of trauma, will be the life my portals return to when they undoubtedly reincarnate back into the human game.

Everything I created with them in my childhood was for our combined contract, and everything I am doing to manage and clear is for all of us to ascend higher. This is how we work together with our bloodline. Everything we experience together in this current lifetime is orchestrated by us before we enter this game. Everything we align to is for us to grow from and our souls to learn from.

Angie sacrificed herself to hold tightly the energy of addiction, so when she transcends and returns I will have done the work to end this behavior and she will then be free of it in her next life. Same with my dad. He is holding tightly to the energy of victim, but this is necessary for me to see so strongly as to heavily persuade me to do and be the opposite. They are playing their roles perfectly, and yes, it's horribly sad to witness but, from my higher consciousness knowing, they are lead characters in us healing our bloodline for the generations to follow.

"What we give energetically is energetically given back to us."

Through my dedication to being of service first to myself so I can be of service to others, I have reached my greatest truth of what I believe this human experience is all about. What this game is, the simulation we are participating in, well, some of us are simply just being puppeted through the simulation.

I believe we are here to create. Many scriptures write of how we are created through the image of God, and what is God? The creator. The creator of all that exists, so therefore, we are here to remember that we are God. The other truths passed through the spiritual world is "one consciousness" or "the law of one", which to me, refers to creation as well.

Everything is conducted through our belief system, aka our consciousness so our role here in the Earth university is to actively participate in the endless evolution of expanding our consciousness, aka evolving our belief system until we reach full ascension.

For me, ascension is evolving from attachment to our physical body into embodying our ethereal body. This is the integration of recognizing "I have a body, but I am not this body. "This body is the vehicle for my ethereal energetic form". We enter into this experience into the 3D realm, which is physical; it is a material world. We entered that realm under a spell of amnesia, as it is designed to be for our soul's education.

Our spirit, aka our soul, our energy, enters Earth University into a physical vessel, containing all of our knowings from the one consciousness who created Earth University but temporarily forgetting them, again by design. Our goal or the master level of the university is to wake up so much from this amnesia to the remembrance that we are not physical. Once we begin remembering this, we begin also aligning to our role as the creator. If everything is energy and energy has no beginning or end, then we hold the information of eternal life. We are energetically connected to the divine information. We are all one which makes us all "the creator".

Now, that is a lot of power to be responsible for, yes I know, which is why many choose to stay enslaved to their physical form and not expand their belief systems—they do not believe they are worthy of such responsibility. To fear our own power is a lower level of consciousness, which is under the control of the 3D matrix system.

Once we take ownership of our power to freely think for ourselves, we can begin moving and shifting our timelines. We can begin envisioning anything; believe it to be true, and it will materialize in front of us. This requires a huge responsibility to stay in our highest frequency because when we drop down from this frequency, even briefly, we are creating at that vibration. For example, if we are in a super high frequency, meditating and envisioning and taking ownership of how our words are spells, which build our reality, and then, say, a close relative transcends, someone who we love dearly, and it's a complete shock. If we claim "death" as real and drop down into victim mode ("I can't believe I'll never see them again. This is the worst thing that could happen to me, I don't know how I will get through this") what you are immediately doing is matching the frequency of fear.

This frequency is 4d, 3D and below, which aligns you to the collective of those realms and the collective fear energy. This vibration disengages you completely from your high frequency of creator and you begin contributing to a lower vibrational collective frequency. There are many different collective simulations occurring; it is our choice which one we contribute to.

As the creator, we accept death isn't real, but transcendence is very real and one of the most beautiful experiences in the human game. No matter the circumstance, there are no accidents; there are no mistakes. The way someone transcends is exactly how they designed their exit from this personal human experience. In place of becoming a victim to the illusionary "death", we have a choice to embody acceptance and be grateful for the moments we shared in our physical forms.

We have many choices all the time. What we choose sets a tone and path, aligning us to the matched frequency of said choice. This act of choosing wisely is the responsibility that many humans are afraid of; to choose wisely and for ourselves requires being in tune with ourselves. This responsibility requires us to reclaim our power from the 3D matrix system which has been controlling our minds and our choices for generations. To do this requires us to fully unplug from the program, to unplug from the collective stories projecting on the tell a vision. To unplug from the spell of mainstream music. From the lyrics that are keeping our minds reciting lower vibrational spells. To unplug from the mental and emotional enslavement of the medical system that grooms us to believe we are sick.

Unplugging from all 3D systems allows us to begin thinking for ourselves. This action is how we reclaim our power and activate the remembrances of how powerful we are. The natural healing abilities we have have been silenced for many generations. Unplugging our minds from the control of a system is how we align to full ascension and beat this human game. It is a process that requires immense grace for ourselves as we begin to disconnect from the illusionary pillars that were "protecting" us.

To fully embody the Creator energy requires us to fully embody our own personal power. When this power is activated, almost never will you desire to go back to the programmed way of life. When we activate our personal power and begin the unplugging, we will "lose" the system attachments that kept us in a comfortable place, and this will feel scary.

The energy you are projecting is now creating a world where you are the main character. This new- found power and our commitment of being of service to ourselves is a beautiful road to freedom. It's not for the weak. The best part about this higher frequency projection is there are others who are also projecting at this vibration, which is a collective of higher dimensional beings, and we are sharing in the creation process together. Many of us have reclaimed our power and are actively creating the most high, most beautiful life for ourselves and our families.

The law is, when more than one has the same vision, the same creation projection, the power is amplified, causing it to materialize faster and in more detail. Hence, why the 3D collective attaches to their news stations—because the information validates their fear energy. It's cyclical: the info validates the fear, the fear creates the scenarios and the scenarios create the fear. Same for higher dimensional: the joy creates the scenario, the scenario creates the joy, the joy emanates through the people, which creates more joy and more belief in the creation process.

Everything in life is cyclical because everything is energy and energy has no beginning or end. It's a constant give and give and give. What we give energetically is energetically given back to us. This is the law of Karma.

"WE ARE THE UNIVERSE."

We are the universe expressing ourselves in a human form. This entire human experience revolves around each one of us individually. Each one of us is having our own personal experience separate from the other, but we are still one and the same.

The law of Karma is not "what you do to others is done to you". The law of Karma is what we energetically project is reflected back to us.

I believe the law of Karma is our moral compass in this human game. What we are experiencing is our compass showing us what direction we are headed based on how we interact with the other players. What energy I embody will be reflected back to me in my daily experiences. What energy I embody will also magnetize to me energies that match that frequency.

If I am in a shit mood and speaking spells of self doubt, hatred for others, angry about my money situations and just in an overall funk, then this day may result in me breaking out with acne on my face because I am speaking poorly of myself. It may result in me running into someone I was just bitching about and having to face them. It may result in me losing my wallet, enhancing my money problems—all because those spells are low vibe and me as the universe created energetically matching situations. It can be as small as those examples or much bigger, depending on how deep you are in the shit mood.

If you have a day of challenges instead of bitching about it and dropping into the victim energy, ask yourself why you created these challenges and what you are needing to learn from them.

Karma is a tool for us. Karma is our friend. The reason why people who do "bad things" have bad things happen to them is because they embody a low vibrational energy, not because "they deserve it". The laws of the universe don't speak grudges or blame or hate. The laws of the universe are simple. Everything is energy; what energy we project is reflected back to us. What spells we recite are creating our reality. What beliefs we have of ourselves, others and life in general is the reality we will experience because our belief system is our consciousness, and our consciousness creates everything we experience.

The universal law does not read through the lines; the universal law operates by energy, so if you say "nothing good ever happens to me", even if you are joking or if you truly believe this, your energy is projecting that this is your truth, and therefore it is what you want to experience for yourself. If you have had a challenging day instead of embodying the victim energy, say to yourself, because you are the universe, "I have everything I need to live my highest timeline" or "Everything conspires for me to be the best version of myself".

Some people use these creation phrases but make the mistake of saying something like "The universe is not against me". We have to be very direct when creating, so this sentence or spell is confusing when it enters the creation realm. It's best to always find the equal opposite highest frequency of every word or situation to be the best creator.

The equal opposite of that spell would be "the universe is working for me". Another example of embodying our master creator energy is reframing all lower vibrational words with the equal opposite. For example, instead of "I don't like when you speak to me like that", say "I prefer to be spoken to like this…." When we are saying what does bring us joy instead of saying what does not bring us joy, we are (1) using our voice to speak our truths and (2) speaking what we want more of not what we don't want more of. This law of creation hears and responds, so be extremely particular what energy you are sending out. Make it a practice to reframe your dislikes for your likes, and you will grow stronger in your truths but also magnetize more of that truth to yourself.

When we begin working with the energy of Karma, we can start to recognize where we have Karmic patterns or have had them. What Karma does is returns to the sender an equally matched energy that can look different each time in hopes of us recognizing what we are sending out so we can then begin correcting it.

Karma is always working in our favor to assist us in our ascension path. We as unity consciousness created Karma to be our tool as our moral compass to help us when we get too far off track. When we are in a karmic loop, we will be in a tornado of matched energies, and it can be very exhausting.

Let's use my dating app stint as an example. Many years ago, I was living in my hometown but also traveling quite a bit, and I hopped on the dating app train in hopes of meeting my forever partner. I chose an app that I thought was not skanky and began my pursuit for partnership. I was also heavily armed in my alcohol, Adderall and cigarette addicTion, keep in mind. I chose men who were not in my hometown because I thought this would prevent me from being imprisoned there if I met my Prince Charming.

In my year of the app game, I went on at least a couple dozen dates, and each one had the same result. They wanted to sleep with me and treat me like a hoe. If we did sleep together, that was it and we never talked again. In these moments, I felt discouraged and pissed off at men (super common theme for me back then). Until my last dating app date who turned into the partner who would be the man I was seeing when I had my car accident that unlocked my dark night of the soul.

He lived five hours from my hometown, and after the accident, I took time off to recover at his place. I got lost in the sauce and moved way too fast, talking about living together and marriage, all of the things that were my karmic patterns. I stayed with him for two weeks before returning home to begin therapy on my back. He paid for the hotel room that I lived in for a month while I was in my hometown.   One week into me being back home, he emailed me with a break up and told me he was sending all of my things to the hotel asap. I was so weak and depressed from the wreck that this just pushed me right over the edge. "How could he leave me in a time like this, how could he do this to me?" I went deep, deep down into victim mode, and it was ugly. It took me a while to enter the other side of that. It took me years of being fully committed to my healing before I could fully dissect this theme of men and recognize my karmic patterns.

I was always drunk on my dates, and this magnetized to me an equal energy with these app men. The drunkenness led to easy access to my sexual energy which led to them not respecting me because, well, hell, I didn't respect myself.

Then I topped it off in my greatest karmic loop of entering a relationship with a much older man who was also very wealthy. This was my all time greatest karmic relationship theme: dating the rich older men who used me as arm candy, and I used them for trips and luxury.

This theme started at age 21 when I dated my first millionaire, who was 60. This karmic cycle lasted almost 20 years and kept me looped in the energy of thirsty, easy and lacking self respect. My fear of being poor again like I was as a child influenced this karmic cycle, but my lack of self love and self respect fueled this very long, very intense karmic cycle.

When I was still in Texas and healing myself physically and emotionally, I processed this cycle, and as karma does, I even brought it back around for me to get another chance to hop back on the train with said ex. He contacted me, needing support while going through a surgery, and I was so close to entering back into the realm of this cycle.

With the help of my bestie and some vintage therapy distractions, I chose myself and told him no. I chose myself and expressed my truth about how I was invested in my healing and I didn't have space to be his support. This broke my karmic cycle; it cleared up my karmic energy and released me from the cycle. It is really quite easy when we can see the cycle. It almost always reeks of lack of self love.

Self love, self worth and self acceptance are key to us reclaiming our power from the external world. These are pillars of strength required for us to stand on while coming back to our divine truths. Lack of self love is the foundation for all of our lower vibrational patterns, and embodying self love is how we reframe all of our lower expressions of self. We are human, after all—our souls have chosen to enter this temporary physical state where our divine energy is confined to a human vessel where we are remembering lower dimensional emotions.

Our souls chose this human game in the Earth University to reactivate how it once was to be a baby soul. To be starting out as part of a grand universal consciousness. Anyone who is here courageously participating in the human game is undoubtedly a strong and evolved soul. We chose to be here doing this thing, and this choice is not for the weak. We are here for a reason—to grow our soul and to assist ourselves in evolving our origin, evolving our contracted family, aka our bloodline. Our family is a team working together to fulfill a contract, aka beat the human game. Our bloodline are our teammates, and we are all working together even when our human selves and our human emotions don't feel this "teamwork". Everything is divinely orchestrated to graduate us with honors from the Earth University. When we return back to our origin, we will return with deeper knowings and deeper truths of who we are as benevolent magical beings.

Printed in Great Britain
by Amazon